BIOGRAPHY FROM
ANCIENT CIVILIZATIONS
LEGENDS, FOLKLORE, AND STORIES OF ANCIENT WORLDS

The Life and Times of

HAMMURABI

Mitchell Lane
PUBLISHERS

P.O. Box 196
Hockessin, Delaware 19707

BIOGRAPHY FROM ANCIENT CIVILIZATIONS
LEGENDS, FOLKLORE, AND STORIES OF ANCIENT WORLDS

Titles
in the Series

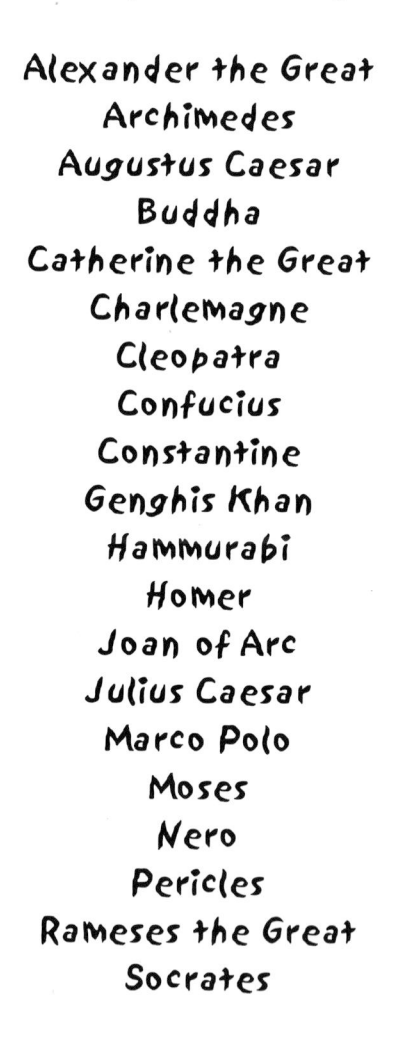

BIOGRAPHY FROM
ANCIENT CIVILIZATIONS
LEGENDS, FOLKLORE, AND STORIES OF ANCIENT WORLDS

The Life and Times of

HAMMURABI

Tamera Bryant

Printing   1   2   3   4   5   6   7   8

Library of Congress Cataloging-in-Publication Data

Bryant, Tamera, 1955–
    The life and times of Hammurabi / by Tamera Bryant.
        p. cm. — (Biography from ancient civilizations)
    Includes bibliographical references and index.
    ISBN 1-58415-338-5 (library bound)
    1. Hammurabi, King of Babylonia—Juvenile literature. 2. Babylonia—History—Juvenile literature. 3. Babylonia—Kings and rulers—Biography—Juvenile literature. I. Title. II. Series.
DS73.35.B794 2005
935'.02'092—dc22
                                                                                        2004030266

ABOUT THE AUTHOR: Tamera Bryant is a writer, educator, activist, and outdoor enthusiast who currently lives in Columbus, Ohio. Her writing includes works for children, teachers, and parents, including the award-winning book, *The Values Book* (Gryphon House). She is currently working on a novel for young adults.

As an educator, Tamera has taught all age levels from infants to adults. Currently she mentors a group of 4th-grade creative writers. She also leads several workshops and visits schools each year to share her innovative approaches to reading and writing.

As an activist, Tamera is involved in politics, education, and environmental action. Her love of the outdoors has led her to work as a volunteer in the National Parks for the past five years. She plans to continue this work as long as she can hike and pitch a tent.

PHOTO CREDITS: Cover, pp. 1, 3—Caveman Art/Sharon Beck; p. 6—Dabar/Sharon Beck; p. 12—American Historical Association; p. 14—Universitat Innsbruck; p. 16—Nasjonalbiblioteket; p. 18—The British Museum; p. 20—Lutheran School; p. 24—Bible Picture Gallery; p. 26—HPS Cambridge; p. 29—MCAH Columbia; p. 31—Ege Universitesi/Sharon Beck; p. 32—Arcimaging; p. 36—Australian National.

PUBLISHER'S NOTE: Since there are no records of actual conversations from Hammurabi's time, all conversations given are fictionalized versions of what might have been said. Many of them are taken from Hammurabi's letters. This story is based on the author's extensive research, which she believes to be accurate. Documentation of such research is contained on page 47.

The internet sites referenced herein were active as of the publication date. Due to the fleeting nature of some web sites, we cannot guarantee they will all be active when you are reading this book.

BIOGRAPHY FROM ANCIENT CIVILIZATIONS
LEGENDS, FOLKLORE, AND STORIES OF ANCIENT WORLDS

The Life and Times of

HAMMURABI

*For Your Information

Sargon was king of ancient Mesopotamia from 2334 B.C.E.* to 2279. He was the first person in recorded history to create an empire. During his 56-year reign, he formed the vast kingdom of Akkad and was known as its great warrior-king. Rulers after Sargon studied and followed his ways.

*B.C.E. ("Before the Common Era") is the same as B.C. (Before Christ) and is expected to replace the religious notation.

CHAPTER
ONE

CHOSEN BY THE GODS

What lands could rival Agade (Akkad)? What king could rival you?
You have no adversary, you are their mighty opponent.
Your opponents' hearts are seared,
They are terrified, and left paralyzed with fear.
Restore (to) them [city]*, field, and lea,
*   the lord (to be your) ally in charge of it.*[1]

The words ran over and over through the young man's mind. They spoke of the great warrior-king Sargon. Sargon had conquered the kingdom of Sumer and built an empire that extended from the Persian Gulf to the Mediterranean Sea (see map on p. 20). He had brought all of Sumer and Akkad under one rule. But that was many years ago. Now the empire was in pieces. Instead of one rule, there were many.

Could the empire be built again? The young man's own father, and even his grandfather before, had dreamed of doing so. They shared a vision of unity, peace, and prosperity not seen since the great Sargon.

*Words in parentheses were added by the translator to help explain the passage. Words in brackets were missing from the original manuscript and filled in by the translator.

Now the young man's father, King Sin-muballit, was very ill. The *asû*, the chief physician, had been tending to him for days. The king's room smelled of the *asû*'s herbs and medicines. There were many of them, but none of them had worked.

"My lord, Hammurabi," an attendant interrupted the young man's thoughts. "The *āšipu* is here. Will you meet him in the king's chambers?"

"Yes. I am on my way. Tell him to confer with the *asû* and the two of them work together on my father's behalf."

Hammurabi was counting on the two doctors. Perhaps the *āšipu* would recite just the right chant to drive the evil demons from the king. This might give the *asû*'s medicines a chance to work. Perhaps the king could be cured and let Hammurabi remain a prince for a while longer.

Sin-mabullit had been king for only twenty years. Hammurabi had been alive almost as many years. From childhood, he had studied in school, called the tablet house. He had studied with the experts to learn about the great kings who had gone before. Hammurabi had watched his father at work. He had listened to the high priests and to his father's many advisors and consultants. Lately, he had even taken on some of the royal duties in preparation for the day that he would be king.

And now that day was here. For even though Hammurabi prayed for his father's cure, in his heart, he knew the outcome. He knew that the gods had already chosen him to sit on his father's throne.

Hammurabi walked from his quarters, known as the House of Succession, to the larger palace and household quarters of his father. As he made his way to his father's side, he realized the weight of his new responsibilities. "The task falls to me," he said to himself. "I will be the one to protect Babylon and raise her up. This city

between the two great rivers, the Tigris and Euphrates, will become the center. She will be the light that spreads across Mesopotamia. The gods have declared so."

And so, Hammurabi, still a teenager, came to the throne of Babylon as the sixth king of the First Dynasty. His sister, Iltani, was at his side. The people embraced him and offered up a prayer for him:

> . . . *before him [ ]* rejoiced at him [ ] embraced him. Your [ ] has determined the destiny. May you be their (savior), exercising lordship over them. May [ ] which has been bestowed on you never cease. You are well-suited for (this), and may its time be prolonged for you. A destiny has been determined for you and you have been called by name; may you have no rival!*[2]

Hammurabi remembered the words of advice to new kings. They gave the advice King Sin-muballit might have offered, if he were still alive.

> *Whoever you may be, governor, prince, or anyone else,*
> *Whom the gods shall name to exercise kingship,*
> *Listen to the words of this stela:*
> *You should not be confounded,*
> *You should not be bewildered,*
> *You should not be afraid, you should not tremble,*
> *Your stance should be firm.*
> *Make your walls trustworthy,*
> *Fill your moats with water.*
> *Your coffers, your grain, your silver, your goods and chattels*
> *[ ] bring into your fortified city.*[3]

Hammurabi took the words to heart. He stood tall and proud. He was already creating a plan. He had inherited a small state—only 80 miles long and 20 miles wide—and it was surrounded by rivals. To

*Square brackets indicate missing text.

the north were the kingdoms of Mari, Ekallatum, and Assyria. The kingdom of Eshnunna was to the east. In the south lay the kingdom of Larsa. These were all larger kingdoms than Babylon, and power shifted from one to the other. Hammurabi's first actions would follow the wisdom of the great kings before. He would fortify the city of Babylon and make her stronger. As king, he would be protector and shepherd. He was not afraid for he knew that he was the agent of the gods.

Anu and Enlil named me, Hammurabi, the exalted prince, the worshipper of the gods, to cause justice to prevail in the land, to destroy the wicked and the evil, to prevent the strong from oppressing the weak, to go forth like the sun over the black-headed people, to enlighten the land and to further the welfare of the people. Hammurabi, the shepherd named by Enlil, am I.[4]

And Hammurabi began his reign over the small kingdom of Babylon.

Gods and Goddesses

The people of Mesopotamia had many gods and goddesses. Each city had its own chief god. To keep the gods happy, people built beautiful temples, called ziggurats, for them. Ziggurats were huge, multi-level towers built of mud bricks. A series of steps, often called the ladder between earth and heaven, led worshipers to the temple on the top tier. A statue of the deity was placed in a special room in the temple. Daily rituals and ceremonies were performed in his or her honor.

Mesopotamian kings believed that they had been chosen by Enlil, who was often referred to as King, Supreme Lord, Father, or Creator. According to one Sumerian legend, no one was allowed to look at Enlil, not even the other gods.

Here are some of the most important gods in Mesopotamia:

Anu was the supreme god who ruled the heavens. His name means "heaven." Anu handed out justice and controlled universal law. With Enlil, Anu bestowed kingships.

Enlil and Ninlil

Enlil was second in command to Anu. He ruled the earth and the forces of nature (especially floods). He was keeper of the Tablet of Destinies that decreed the fates of gods and men. Enlil was the father of the moon god Nana, the sun god Shamash, the weather god Adad, and the love goddess Ishtar. Enlil was also called Bel.

Enki ruled the oceans, streams, and rivers. He was associated with wisdom, sorcery, and skilled crafts. Enki was also called Ea.

Marduk was the god of Babylon. He represented the forces of good over evil. People prayed to Marduk when they wanted his protection. Marduk's main temple was the Esagila in Babylon.

Shamash was the sun god who ruled over justice. He was known as the light that banishes darkness, that sees all things from heaven.

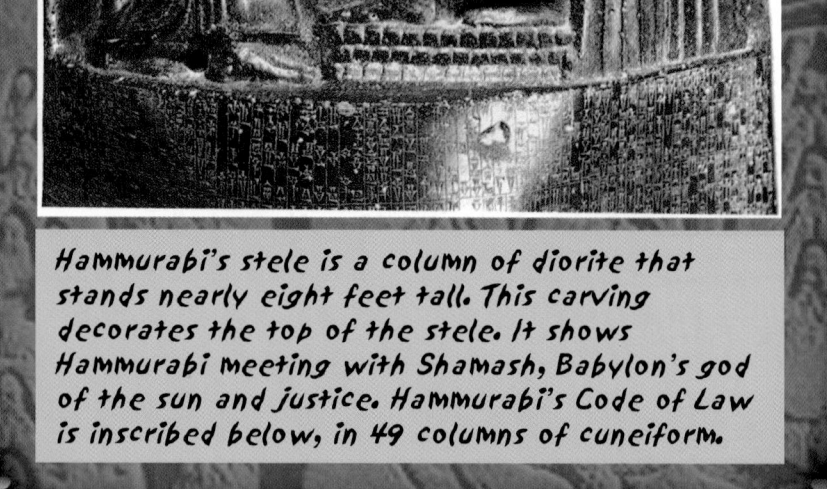

Hammurabi's stele is a column of diorite that stands nearly eight feet tall. This carving decorates the top of the stele. It shows Hammurabi meeting with Shamash, Babylon's god of the sun and justice. Hammurabi's Code of Law is inscribed below, in 49 columns of cuneiform.

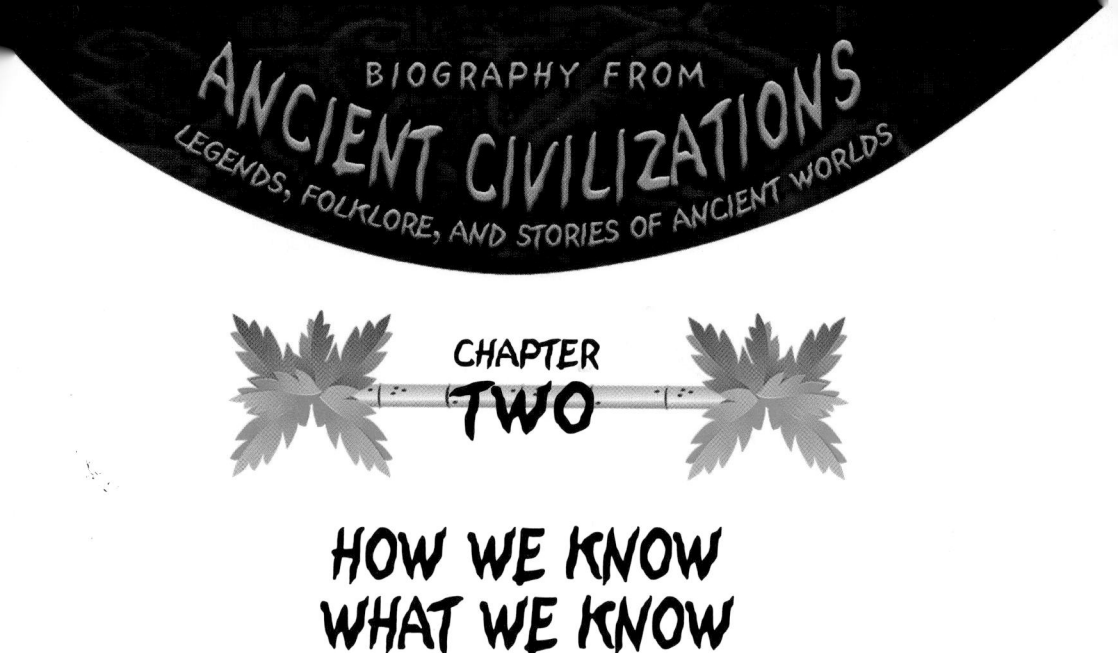

CHAPTER
TWO

HOW WE KNOW WHAT WE KNOW

Hammurabi lived in Babylon (now part of modern day Iraq) more than 3,700 years ago. There are no photographs, no film, and no sound recordings of any part of his life. Of course, those things hadn't been invented when Hammurabi was alive. The city of Babylon, where Hammurabi spent his life, no longer exists. Hundreds of years after Hammurabi's death, a new Babylon was built on top of it.

So how do we know anything about Hammurabi's life? How do we even know that such a man really lived so long ago?

We know because archaeologists tell us. Archaeologists— scientists armed with maps, picks, shovels, brushes, and brooms— have excavated, or dug up, the areas around Babylon and other ancient cities. In their excavating, they have discovered important clues about the life and times of Hammurabi. The three most important are:

1. Hammurabi's year date formula
2. Hammurabi's letters
3. Hammurabi's stele

Temples were among the largest and most important buildings in Mesopotamia. Kings built them to show their gratitude and loyalty to the gods. Thrones were usually placed on top of a large dais, or platform, like this one. This showed that the god was above all others in the room, inspiring both loyalty and fear in visitors.

Hammurabi's year date formula is really just a list of all the years that Hammurabi was king of Babylonia. Each year has a number and a description that tells about a major act or accomplishment, usually of the year before. For example, we know from the year date formula that, in his third year as king, Hammurabi "made a magnificent throne dais for the temple of Nanna in Ur."[1] Significant acts in other years include building and restoring temples, digging canals, constructing city walls, and fighting wars. Some years have more than one description.

Kings before and after Hammurabi also wrote their own lists, so we have some information about Hammurabi's father as well. This information helps us fill in "knowledge gaps" about ancient Babylonian society.

Archaeologists have found about 150 of Hammurabi's letters. In the letters, it is obvious that Hammurabi took a personal interest in all aspects of Babylonian life. He sent letters directing the cleaning out of canals, the shipment of wood, and the delivery of dates and sesame seed. Most of the letters are addressed to Sin-Idinnam, his deputy in Larsa. Larsa is where the letters were found. Others have been uncovered in Mari and other cities. In addition to Hammurabi's letters, archaeologists have found letters from other kings and ambassadors. These tell us a little more about life of that time.

How could a letter survive for more than 3,700 years? Letters from ancient Mesopotamia did not look like letters do today. They weren't written on paper or even with a pen or pencil. They were written in soft clay tablets with a reed. When the clay hardened, the letters were preserved. In some cities, like Mari, whole libraries of these clay tablets have been discovered. They are written in a text known as cuneiform.

Archaeologists had been uncovering clay tablets containing cuneiform since the late seventeenth century. A German teacher named Georg Friedrich Grotefend worked on decoding the ancient symbols in the late 1700s and early 1800s. In 1825, an Englishman named Henry Rawlinson made a huge **INITIAL** He found carved inscriptions in Iran. They were wr**HERE**three languages: Babylonian, Elamite, and Old Persian. Rawlinson figured out that all the texts told the same story. He knew enough Old Persian to decipher the text in that language. Then he used that to decode the other two languages. It took several years, but we could now read and translate cuneiform.

Finally, we have Hammuarbi's stele, a tall stone column that has Hammurabi's law code inscribed in it. <u>The code is the longest piece of text still surviving from the Old Babylonian period</u>. It was discovered in southwestern Iran in 1902. A team of French archaeologists, led by M. J. de Morgan, were excavating near the town of Susa. They found several pieces of a stone called black diorite. The pieces fit together to form a large block. On one side was

*Cuneiform is the oldest form of writing.
Mesopotamian scribes used cuneiform characters
to record stories, daily events, business dealings,
and movements of the stars and planets. This clay
tablet has two columns of writing, and there are
49 lines in each column. These record some of
Hammurabi's law code.*

a carved relief of Hammurabi with Babylon's sun god. The other
sides contained long columns of cuneiform text. These turned out to
be the Law Code of Hammurabi. The stele was in Susa and not
Babylon because the Elamites had stolen it and carried it off. They
probably took it as a sign of a victory in battle sometime around
1200 B.C.E.

Cuneiform

FYI
For Your Info

A	B	C	D	E	F	G	H

I	J	K	L	M	N	O	P

Q	R	S	T	U	V	W	X

Y	Z

Cuneiform is the earliest form of writing. It was invented by the Sumerians in Mesopotamia, possibly as early as six thousand years ago, so that they could keep better business records. Using stiff reeds, they drew pictures of cattle, sheep, and barley in soft clay to show numbers or amounts of each. Over time, the pictures evolved into symbols and then into wedge-shaped characters. The word *cuneiform* means "wedge-shaped."

The uses of writing also evolved. Cuneiform provided a way for kings and other officials to communicate. It was no longer necessary to trust a messenger to remember the message. Kings could send letters written in clay.

The clay tablets used for writing cuneiform were made in different shapes and sizes. Most were flat, but some were round and hollow like vases. Most of the letters that have been found are flat and oblong. They are two to three inches wide, three to four inches long, and about one inch thick. Clay envelopes were made to carry the tablets containing important messages from government officials.

There were more than 600 cuneiform signs. This made cuneiform a difficult system to learn. Young boys went to school to learn how to read and write. They also learned how to mix and prepare the clay and form it into tablets. They trained to be professional writers called scribes. Only boys from wealthy families could afford to go to school.

Because so few people could read or write, those who could scribe, held a respected position in society. They were extremely valuable to kings, priests, and other officials. Hammurabi, like other Babylonian kings, always used the same scribe. All his letters are in the same careful handwriting.

Shamshi-Adad ruled Assyria from about 1813 B.C.E. to 1781. Before taking the throne, he spent time in Babylon as an exile. The time he spent in Babylon instilled a sense of fondness and loyalty toward the city. Shamshi-Adad did not forget the hospitality of the Babylonians. He kept his alliance with Hammurabi until his death.

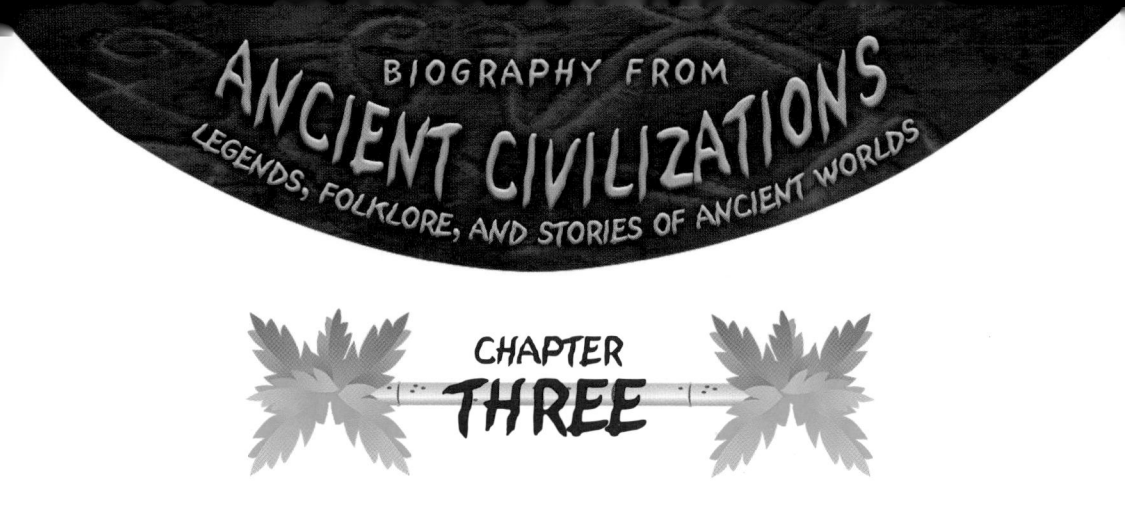
CHAPTER
THREE

A PRACTICAL KING

Two thousand years before Hammurabi, farmers began moving into Mesopotamia. Known as the Fertile Crescent, the land stretched out between the Tigris and Euphrates rivers. The combination of sun, soil, and water made the area a good place for growing crops and raising animals. People who had once been nomads began to settle down.

The population of Mesopotamia grew. People saw the benefits of building communities and cities. They learned to share in the work and in the rewards. Before, one person had to learn many different skills to survive. Now several people could divide the work. Some people farmed; some raised sheep or cattle. Others became builders, bakers, artisans, merchants, and sailors. People started depending on each other.

One of the cities that grew during this time was Babylon. By 3500 B.C.E., Babylon was a thriving city of business, trade, art, and architecture. Like other cities then and now, it began to spread out. Inside the main city were businesses, homes, and temples. Outside the city lay farms and smaller towns and communities. Babylon's rulers claimed parts of the outlying areas. The city and its

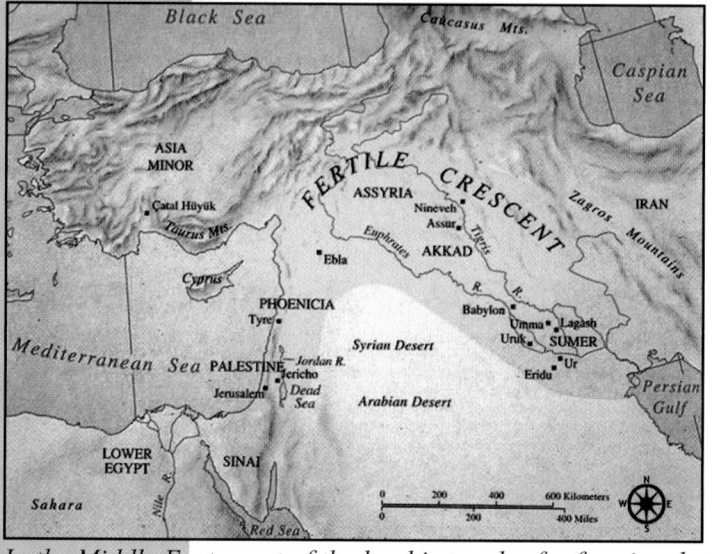

In the Middle East, most of the land is too dry for farming, but the region known as the Fertile Crescent is different. It stretches from the Mediterranean Sea to the Persian Gulf. The Tigris and Euphrates Rivers run through it, creating a rich, food-growing area. The Greeks called it Mesopotamia, which means "between the rivers."

surrounding towns became a city-state, something like a very small country.

When Hammurabi became king, there were a number of these city-states in Mesopotamia. Many of them were bound to each other by treaties. In these treaties, rulers agreed not to attack each other. They also promised to help each other in case anyone else attacked. Hammurabi was familiar with these treaties and alliances. He saw right away that Babylon would benefit from keeping the treaties already in place. He also negotiated new treaties.

A king named Shamshi-Adad was the ruler of Assyria, a large region that stretched both north and west of Babylon. Hammurabi approached Shamshi-Adad soon after he became king.

"Why should I form an alliance with you?" Shamshi-Adad asked Hammurabi. "I command all of Assyria."

"Because Babylon has been good to you," answered Hammurabi. "Years ago, when the Eshnunna army drove you from the city of Ekallatum, where did you find refuge? Babylon. When you returned to your city to take it back, where did your fighting men come from? Babylon. Babylon is your friend. I wish it to remain so."

"You are right," said Shamshi-Adad. "Let us agree then. Babylon and Assyria are in alliance."

"And what of Ekallatum now, and Mari? They are also in your control," Hammurabi said.

"My sons, Ishme-Dagan and Yasmah-Adad, are in place in those cities. They control those areas," answered Shamshi-Adad.

"Yes, but do you not control your sons?" Hammurabi smiled.

"So be it," said Shamshi-Adad. "We are all in alliance. No one from northern Mesopotamia will harm Babylon. In exchange, of course, you must not look to the north with envy. You and your armies will protect and support Shamshi-Adad and all the lands of Assyria."

Hammurabi agreed. He now had the powerful Shamshi-Adad on his side. This alliance gave Hammurabi something very valuable: time. He spent that time getting Babylon's affairs in order and making sure that his control there was secured. He built up the city, reinforcing its walls, maintaining its irrigation system, and constructing new temples for the gods. As each project was completed, Hammurabi gained more respect and more praise:

Enki has esteemed him truly in the shrine, the august place— the king who loves purification rites and is well-suited to the pure divine powers, the king who is skilled in the precious plans, who is reverent, eloquent and deft (?), the shepherd, favorite of lord Nunamnir and beloved of mother Ninlil, . . . who is cherished by holy Damgalnuna: the good shepherd Hammurabi.

*The king has . . . everything in the shrine Ekisznuğal.
Hammurabi, . . . has restored the purification rites, plans, and
divine powers. . . . He will stand there before you, . . . fulfilling . . .
all your requirements.*[1]

Records of Hammurabi's works were inscribed on clay tablets.
Each year was named for one or more of the king's accomplishments:

Year 1   Hammurabi became king

Year 2   Hammurabi, the king, established justice / released
force labor in his land

Year 3a   Hammurabi made a magnificent throne dais for the
temple of Nanna in Ur / the Ekisznugal in Babylon

Year 3b   Hammurabi built for Nanna his temple in Babylon

Year 4   Hammurabi restored the great wall of the nunnery and
built the city wall of Sziramah / Isziramah

Year 5   Hammurabi made (a statue called) "the lord is the
decision maker of heaven and earth"

Year 6   Hammurabi made a throne for Ninpirig[2]

Year 7 was marked by a different kind of inscription. In that year,
Hammurabi seized Uruk and Isin, cities south of Babylon and
controlled by Rim-Sin of Larsa. Once he had proven his growing
power to Rim-Sin, Hammurabi formed a treaty with him. This treaty
assured him that Rim-Sin would not retaliate.

Now Hammurabi had protection from both the north and the
south. Two years later he conquered the small country of Emutbal.
He took the city of Malgia two years after that. Then he returned to
the work of digging canals and building strong walls around his cities,
temples, and palaces.

"Lord Hammurabi, you have been successful in your efforts to
expand the borders of Babylon. Why have you stopped?" asked a
military advisor.

"Babylon has other matters to attend. Canals must be kept up so that the farmers have enough water. Walls must be put up to protect us from unexpected enemies. Temples must be built so that the gods continue to smile on us. Work goes on all around you," answered Hammurabi.

"Yes, lord," the advisor answered, "but the others will not stand by and wait while you dig and build. Ishme-Dagan, ruler of Ekallatum, grows restless and wants to prove himself to his father, Shamshi-Adad. Yasmah-Adad of Mari wants to become bigger than his brother Ishme-Dagan. Rim-Sin of Larsa will certainly break your treaty soon. I am worried that alliances will shift, and not in our favor."

"It is all right," Hammurabi said. "I have something the others do not: patience."

Six years later, Hammurabi's patience paid off. Both Shamshi-Adad, ruler of Assyria, and his son Yasmah-Adad, ruler of Mari, were killed. Zimri-Lim, the son of an earlier Mari king, returned to that city and took it over. Hammurabi wasted no time. He knew that rulers in Eshnunna and Elam had their eyes on Mari. They planned to take advantage of the confusion there and conquer the city for themselves. That would leave them too strong. Hammurabi was quick to form his own treaty with Zimri-Lim. He offered military support and protection to Mari. In exchange, Zimri-Lim would provide the same to Babylon.

And so a potential war was avoided. Hammurabi could go back to the business of Babylon.

He may have been patient in foreign affairs, but in his day-to-day actions, Hammurabi seemed to be constantly in motion. There was always something to be done, something to be handled, from canals to be built to markets to be kept open. And Hammurabi kept his hand in all of it. Perhaps he did not trust others to do a job as well as

Hammurabi's Babylon does not exist any longer. Years after Hammurabi's death, a new Babylon was built on top of the old one. The city had eight gates. This one was called the Ishtar Gate. King Nebuchadnezzar II had it built to honor the goddess Ishtar. The walls were covered with blue glazed tiles and carvings of dragons and bulls.

he could. Perhaps he took pride in being a king who showed such personal interest in his subjects. Perhaps he enjoyed knowing all the details of the world around him.

Whatever the reason, Hammurabi took on projects and situations that other kings might have delegated to others. He concentrated on strengthening Babylon. All the while, he kept a close and careful watch on his allies. The last thing he wanted was for them to become enemies.

Twelve years passed in peace. Alliances remained in place for the most part. Some shifts occurred, but the kings were fairly balanced in their power and influence:

> *There is no king who by himself is strongest. Ten or fifteen kings follow Hammurabi of Babylon, as many follow Rim-Sin of Larsa, Ibal-pi-El of Eshnunna and Amut-pi-El of Qatna, while twenty kings follow Yarim-Lim of Yamhad.*[3]

That was about to change.

Irrigation and Farming

Mesopotamia's most important crop was barley. Farmers also grew apples, dates, pomegranates, grapes, onions, leeks, and turnips. Dates were especially important because they could be dried and stored so that they could be eaten all year.

Mesopotamia was hot, with little rain. Only the annual flooding of the Tigris and Euphrates provided enough water to grow food at all. There was another problem, though. The floods came when crops were already growing in the fields. Too much water destroyed them.

A Canal

Mesopotamians solved this problem by building a complex system of canals and dikes. Dikes, raised mounds along the riverbeds, kept the rivers from overflowing into the fields. The water was channeled into canals, or ditches, that carried it from the river to storage reservoirs. Farmers could control the flow of water into their fields. This irrigation system served two essential purposes: (1) It controlled the flooding rivers and kept the fields from flooding, and (2) it carried water to areas that would otherwise be too dry for farming.

The river waters carried sand and clay particles called silt. As silt settled, it was deposited in the canals. To keep the canals from filling with the silt, farmers and canal workers had to regularly dig out the canals. This was extremely hard work. Even the smallest canals, called branch canals, were at least 3 1/2 to 5 feet wide and 7 feet deep, and they could be more than a mile long.

Mesopotamian kings like Hammurabi believed that building and keeping canals was a sacred duty. When an especially large-scale canal project was completed, it was important enough to be listed in the king's year date formula.

In Babylonian mythology, Marduk fights an army of demons led by the goddess Tiamat. After he hunts down Tiamat and kills her, he is crowned as the supreme god of Babylon. Each year Babylonians celebrated a New Year festival in Marduk's honor. During the festival, the king would kneel before a statue of Marduk and vow that he was a good ruler.

CHAPTER
FOUR

AN AMBITIOUS KING

The peace between the city-states was uneasy. No king trusted another absolutely. To ease suspicions, they sent representatives to stay in rival cities. These representatives were called ambassadors, but they were actually spies. Their job was to collect information about troop movements, shifting alliances, and other happenings. Then they would send the information back to their king by messenger. Sometimes a spy or a messenger would work for more than one king:

> *Whenever Hammurabi is perturbed by some matter, he always sends for me, and I go to him wherever he is. He tells me whatever is troubling him, and all of the important information which he tells me I continually report to my lord.*[1]

The "lord" in this case was Zimri-Lim of Mari. Although he and Hammurabi were in alliance, it seems neither king was completely content with the agreement. Still, each of them had kept his word for more than ten years.

Rim-Sin of Larsa had a similar arrangement with Hammurabi. Each had agreed to respect the other and to defend him whenever necessary. If any king failed in his commitment to another, the balance of power could shift. The fear was always that one king might become powerful enough to overthrow the others. Because of this, kings kept each other in check. Often they did this through their alliances, but sometimes they did so by ignoring them.

In Hammurabi's twenty-ninth year, Elam and Eshnunna joined their armies. Hammurabi believed they were planning to invade a Babylonian city on the Tigris. He sent word for Rim-Sin of Larsa to come to his aid with troops. The troops did not come. Instead Hammurabi received a letter from Rim-Sin:

> *Tell my lord: Your servant Yarim-Addu sends the following message:*
>
> *Two officials of King Hammurabi, Tabelimatim and Sinbelaplim, who for a long time were staying in the city of Maskansabra, have arrived here in Babylon; four men from Larsa, riding on donkeys, are escorting them. I obtained intelligence of the message they are carrying (from the king of Larsa): they are supposed to tell Hammurabi the following: As to the soldiers for whom you keep writing me, the reason why I did not send them to you is that I have heard that the enemy's intentions are directed against another country. But I am still holding the soldiers in readiness; should the enemy turn against you, my soldiers will come to your aid. On the other hand, should the enemy turn against me, your soldiers should come to my aid." This is the message which King Rim-Sin sent to Hammurabi.[2]*

But the armies of Elam and Eshnunna did invade, and war started. Hammurabi's soldiers, even without the promised help of Rim-Sin, were fierce, and they defeated the enemy forces. However, Hammurabi was not happy with the way Rim-Sin had broken their treaty. To make matters worse, Hammurabi learned that Rim-Sin had sent raiding parties to other Babylonian territories and had taken Babylonian prisoners. Hammurabi tried to negotiate with Rim-Sin at

The Tigris River is about 1,150 miles long. It flows from eastern Turkey until it joins with the Euphrates River in southern Iraq. It delivers much needed water to the region known as the Fertile Crescent. The name Tigris comes from Old Persia and means "the fast one."

first, but then he received news that changed his mind. Rim-Sin was preparing 270 boats for a large-scale attack.

It was time for action. Hammurabi called for the *baru*, the diviners who read signs and omens, for guidance. They would perform the omen ritual and ask Marduk for answers. When they arrived, Hammurabi presented them a sheep to be sacrificed. This was part of the ritual.

Hammurabi explained how Rim-Sin had betrayed him. Then he asked, "What would the great Marduk have me do?"

The *baru* called to Marduk, asking him the question. "Oh, mighty Marduk, write your answer on the entrails (intestines) of this sheep so that our great king, Hammurabi, will know your way."

The sheep was slaughtered and the *baru* examined its insides from top to bottom. They studied each organ for marks and changing colors.

"Here," said one. "*Kakku*, the weapon."

"Yes, I see it. It points to the right," said the other.

"What is its meaning?" demanded Hammurabi.

"To the right, the omen is favorable for war. You will be victorious."

A prayer to Marduk (?) for Hammurabi:
> *May Lugal-Šubur place on your head the desert crown of kingship! May Enki, the lord of life, . . . life, and in the E-unir, the house of the plans of heaven and earth which rides upon all the divine powers, may he cover your priestly headdress in awe and splendor! May he make the divine powers of kingship resplendent for you, and fit you up forever with the plans appropriate to the rank of a priest! May he gently recite for you life-giving incantations, bestowing in addition a long-lived destiny; may the uttering of your name delight Enki as much as the uttering of his own name! May he reward you with wisdom and intelligence! May your royal name be as something unchangeable! May father Enki prolong the years of your life, and may he grant you lordship over every one of the foreign lands. O Hammurabi, my king!*[3]

Hammurabi stopped all talks with Rim-Sin. He began planning his own attack against Larsa. He would invade first at Mashkan-shapir, Larsa's second largest city. His soldiers, who had fought so well against the Elamites, would be victorious. And he, Hammurabi, claiming Marduk as his guide, would be merciful to the conquered. And that is just how it happened. The Babylonian forces took the city of Mashkan-shapir, but they did not destroy it. The people of the city were so grateful that they joined Hammurabi's army.

The victory likely strengthened Hammurabi's confidence. Certainly it strengthened the empire, and Hammurabi moved on to Larsa. His growing forces of chariots, spear throwers, and archers

In Babylonian mythology, Shamash was the god of the sun and of justice. The people believed that Shamash could see everything. Here, Shamash is meeting with Hammurabi. Sun rays come from the shoulders of Shamash. He holds a ring out to Hammurabi. Hammurabi is wearing the royal headpiece of a king. His raised hand shows that he is praying to Shamash for guidance and wisdom.

stormed the city of Rim-Sin. The fighting went on for quite some time. Finally, Hammurabi used his knowledge of waterways and canal-building to bring the war to an end. He ordered canals destroyed and the Euphrates River dammed to cut off the water supply to Larsa. The city surrendered. The name given to that year said it all:

> *Year Hammurabi the king, trusting An and Enlil who marches in front of his army and with the supreme power which the great gods have given to him, destroyed the troops of Emutbal and subjugated its king Rim-Sin and brought Sumer and Akkad to dwell under his authority.*[4]

Now the balance of power had definitely shifted. Hammurabi was becoming too strong, and his northern rivals felt threatened. Elam and Eshnunna were regrouping and rebuilding their armies. They wanted to stop Hammurabi from becoming any stronger. Hammurabi sent word to his old ally Zimri-Lim of Mari, asking for

The Euphrates River is almost 1,700 miles long. It flows from Turkey, through Syria, and then eventually joins with the Tigris River in Iraq. The name Euphrates comes from Old Persia and means "good to cross over."

reinforcements. Zimri-Lim, like Rim-Sin, ignored Hammurabi's request. He, too, was hoping that Hammurabi would be stopped.

Even without Zimri-Lim's help, Hammurabi's army was able to crush the Elamites when they attacked. This time it was for good. Now Hammurabi could not be stopped. He moved on toward Mari. Just as he had attacked Rim-Sin in the south, he went after Zimri-Lim in the north. In the end, Mari, like Larsa, fell under Hammurabi's rule.

There was one region left to take: Assyria. Hammurabi moved through the northern regions of Mesopotamia, taking one city after another. By his thirty-seventh year, all of Mesopotamia was under his influence. It had taken him less than ten years to secure the entire empire.

Hammurabi remembered the day of his father's death. The questions he had then were now being answered. Hammurabi had rebuilt the empire his father and grandfather had dreamed of. All of Sumer was again under one rule. Hammurabi declared himself the king "of the four quarters of the world." The land was his. Now he would have to work on rebuilding peace and prosperity for the people.

A top priority was to repair and rebuild damaged canals. The people depended on the water the canals delivered to their homes and farms. They also used the canals for the boats that carried trade goods between cities. As he had in the past, Hammurabi supervised these projects himself, sending instructions to deputies scattered across the empire. Sin-Idinnam was his deputy in Larsa.

Unto Sin-idinnam say:
> *Thus sayeth Hammurabi. Thou shalt call out the men who hold lands along the banks of the Damanum-canal that they may clear out the Damanum-canal. Within the present month shall they complete the work of clearing out the Damanum-canal.*
> *The canal which has been cleared out hath not been cleared out as far as the city of Erech, and therefore [boats?] cannot enter the city. . . . This work is not too great for the men that are at thy disposal. . . . When, therefore, thou shalt behold this tablet, with the company of men at thy disposal thou shalt clear out the canal within the city of Erech in three days. After that thou shalt do the work concerning which I have written unto thee.*[5]

It seems no project was too small or too large for Hammurabi. Whatever the task at hand, he would organize and oversee it. In his letters, he sent his orders for work as grand as constructing temples for the gods and as mundane as shearing sheep:

Mendibum, Bel-da[ ], and Masparum have written, saying "The men who have been appointed unto us for the sheep-shearing are too

few for the sheep." After this fashion have they written. Thou shalt therefore appoint a strong body of men that the shearing may be speedily finished.[6]

Year names for this peaceful period of building and progress included the names of temples, new city walls, large canals, shrines, and statues. When an important project was completed, an official inscription was written:

For Shamash, the lord of heaven and earth, his king, Hammurabi, the minister of Anu, the servant of Bel, the beloved Shamash, the shepherd who delighteth Marduk's heart, the mighty king, the king of Babylon, the king of Sumer and Akkad, the king of the four quarters of the world, the king who hath built anew the shrines of the great gods,—when Shamash gave unto him Sumer and Akkad to rule, and entrusted their scepter to his hands, he did (Hammurabi) build for Shamash, the lord who is the protector of his life, the temple E-babbar, his beloved temple, in Larsa, the city of his rule.[7]

It was a time of movement, action, and building up. It was also a time of thoughtfulness. More than anything, Hammurabi wanted to be the "shepherd," the peaceful protector of a peaceful people. For him that meant establishing a strong rule and a strict but just law. One would handle larger enemies that wanted to harm Babylonia. The other would handle conflicts between people going about daily life.

Craft and Construction

Mesopotamians were expert artisans and craft workers. Babylonian metalworkers were especially important during Hammurabi's decade of war. The main metal was bronze, which was a mixture of copper and tin. Bronze was a much harder, stronger metal than either of the metals used to make it. This made it a much better material to use for arrowheads, spearheads, and helmets.

Another skill that grew in importance during this time was brick making. Other cultures, like the Palestinians, used stone for building, but stones were rare in Mesopotamia. The Mesopotamians formed bricks from clay and then dried them. Bricks for houses were baked in the sun to make them hard. Bricks for more important buildings, like palaces and ziggurats, were fired in large ovens, called kilns. The oven firing was expensive because wood for the fires had to be imported. But the oven-fired bricks were stronger and more durable.

The clay for the bricks was actually a mixture of clay and straw. The straw helped hold the clay together and made it stronger. Brick makers pressed the mixture into wooden molds. In the time of Hammurabi, these molds—and the bricks made with them—were squares about 14 inches on each side.

Ziggurat

The ziggurats were built with these small bricks. Consider that the most common size for a ziggurat base was about 135 feet by 160 feet and as many as 70 feet high. From the base, the sides were built up in tiers, or levels. Each level could be another 20 feet high. Imagine how many mud bricks were needed to build one ziggurat!

This piece of art came from the ancient city of Larsa, where a dignitary named Awil-Nanna dedicated it to the god Amurru "for the life of Hammurabi." The small bronze statue probably is Hammurabi. He is wearing the royal headpiece. His hand is raised in prayer. The small bowl in front would have been for offerings.

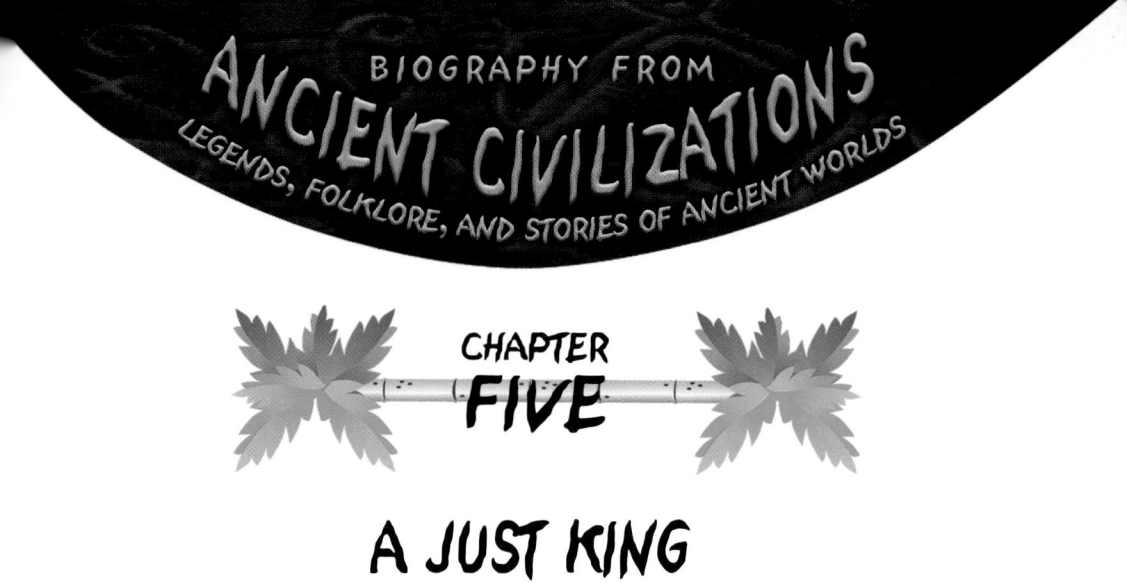

CHAPTER
FIVE

A JUST KING

Hammurabi had conquered "the four quarters of the world." He now ruled a vast empire that included all of Mesopotamia. The people of that empire, although they shared many things in common, had different backgrounds and practiced different customs. They were not yet one people.

Hammurabi thought of himself as the "shepherd" of his people. It was his duty to protect them as well as lead them. The well-being of his subjects, especially the poor and oppressed, was of great concern to him. Over the years, he had made laws to protect his people. Now he believed that he needed to make those laws more permanent and more public.

*"I will collect the laws in one place as a record of what is just and as a promise that justice will prevail,"** proclaimed Hammurabi.

"How will you do this?" his deputy asked.

"I will carve the law in stone."

"My lord, have not others before you collected laws? Surely our customs are similar enough, and the people are already familiar with them. Why do you not rely on those?"

*All quotes in italic refer to when Hammurabi is speaking.

"If Babylonia is to have public order, we must move beyond custom. Babylon will have a code of law, a system to aid the people. It will include justice and be written in the language of the land. Should any accused man be brought before me or my court, and be guilty, he will know his punishment and its harshness from the code. The punishment will be set with the crime," Hammurabi answered. *"Anu and Enlil named me, Hammurabi, . . . to cause justice to prevail in the land, to destroy the wicked and the evil, to prevent the strong from oppressing the weak, to go forth like the sun over the black-headed people, to enlighten the land and to further the welfare of the people."*[1]

"And what of the man who accuses another unjustly? If punishments are recorded, will that be too dangerous? What is to stop one man from lying about another? For example, you have said 'If a man practices robbery and is captured, that man shall be put to death.' If a man wants another man dead, he would have only to say he caught the man robbing him."

Hammurabi answered, *"If a man bears false witness in a case, or does not establish the testimony that he has given, if that case is a case involving life, that man shall be put to death. [Law 3]* This will be written in the code. Also, if a man brings an accusation against another man, charging him with murder, but cannot prove it, the accuser shall be put to death."* [Law 1]

"These punishments are strict, my lord. Why not impose a fine or send a man to jail?"

"These punishments are equal to the crimes they punish. Punishment must serve justice. If (a man) bears false witness concerning grain or money, he shall himself bear the penalty imposed in that case." [Law 4]

"That is fair. If I may ask, what other matters will the law code address?"

"If it is to protect and govern all of Babylonia, then it must consider all matters of Babylonian society."

"Marriage and divorce?"

---

*All bracketed text at the end of quotes refer to the "Laws of Hammurabi." They contain the Law with their coordinating number (see note 1 in Chapter Notes).

"Yes, and adoption and other family matters. Women and children must be protected from poverty and neglect. A man may divorce his wife, but if he has children, he must continue to support both his wife and his children."

"Private property?"

"If a man practices robbery and is captured, that man shall be put to death. If the robber is not captured, the man who was robbed shall, in the presence of god, make a . . . statement of his loss, and the city . . . shall compensate (pay) him for whatever he lost." [Laws 22 and 23]

"And injury? What if a man breaks another man's bone?"

"They shall break his bone." [Law 197]

"Ah, what if a man breaks the bone of a man's slave?"

"He shall pay one-half the slave's price." [Law 199]

"What if a man strikes another without intent?"

"He shall pay for the physician. If the man he strikes is a citizen, he shall pay the physician five shekels of silver. If the man he strikes is a slave, he shall pay the physician two shekels." [Laws 206, 216, and 217]

"What if a physician operates on a man and causes the man's death?"

"They shall cut off his hand." [Law 218]

"What of our irrigation canals? Will law govern those as well?"

"Society depends on it. All our economy is based on the movement and storage of water. If the canals are not maintained, crop lands will either dry up or be flooded by spring rains. If no barley grows, what will we trade for copper and wood? Yes, canals and dikes must be kept in good working order."

"But what if a man neglects to keep his dike and does not strengthen it, and a break is made and the water carries away the farmland?"

"That man shall replace the grain which has been damaged." [Law 53]

"But what if he is not able to because his own grain is damaged?"

"They shall sell him and his goods. The farmers whose grain the water has carried away shall divide the money from the sale." [Law 54]

"A farmer should not neglect his work."

"*Anyone with a responsibility should take care. People depend on each other. They must be able to trust that work is done properly and with care and attention.*"

"What if a builder builds a house and does not make it sound? What if the wall cracks?"

"*The builder shall strengthen that wall at his own expense.*" [Law 233]

"What if the building collapses and causes the death of the owner?"

"*The builder shall be put to death.*" [Law 229]

"What if a builder builds a house for a man and it is sound?"

"*The owner shall give the builder two shekels of silver per* sar *of house as the builder's fee.*" [Law 228]

"So the law code sets wages and fees as well as punishments?"

"*If a man hires a field laborer, he shall pay him eight* gur *of grain per year. A herdsman shall get six* gur.*" [Laws 257 and 258]

"My lord, I can pose no more problems for you to answer."

"*Call the stone worker and the scribe.*"

Hammurabi's Law Code was carved in a stone column called a stele. When it was completed, it stood nearly eight feet tall. It contained 282 laws written in 49 columns that covered all sides of the column. At the very top, the sculptor carved a likeness of Hammurabi at the throne of Shamash, god of justice and the sun. Shamash is holding out a rod and a ring to Hammurabi as symbols of royal authority. A prologue introduced the Code, and an epilogue followed the 282 laws. The epilogue explained Hammurabi's reasons for his stele:

These are the just laws which Hammurabi, the wise king, established and by which he gave the land stable support and good government. Hammurabi, the perfect king, am I. I was not careless, nor was I neglectful of the black-headed people, whose rule Enlil presented and Marduk delivered to me. . . .

In order that the strong might not oppress the weak, that justice be given to the orphan and the widow, in Babylon, the city whose turrets Anu and Enlil raised, the Esagila, the temple whose foundations are firm as heaven and earth, for the pronouncing of judgments in the land, for the rendering of decisions for the land, and to give justice to the oppressed, my weighty words I have written upon my monument, and in the presence of my image as king of justice have I established it.

"Let any oppressed man, who has a cause, come before my image as king of justice! Let him read the inscription on my monument! Let him give heed to my weighty words! And may my monument enlighten him as to his cause and may he understand his case! May he set his heart at ease!" [Epilogue].

The final years of Hammuarbi's rule were peaceful. Hammurabi enjoyed his role as "the powerful king, the sun of Babylon, who caused light to go forth over the lands of Sumer and Akkad; the king who caused the four quarters of the world to render obedience." He continued to oversee building projects as he had always done. There was always canal work to be done, and some of Babylonia's cities still needed repair. One of his last construction projects was a wall around the city of Sippar.

Hammurabi's story ended as it had begun. In his final days, he let his mind wander back to the day that he had taken the throne. He had fulfilled his dream from that day. The vision of his father and his grandfather was realized. Now he was a sick man, and his own son, Samsuiluna, called for the *asû* and *āšipu*.

Thus saith Samsuiluna:
The king, my father, is sick and I sat myself on the throne in order to [protect] the country.[2]

After 43 years as king and protector, Hammurabi was dead.

FYI
For Your Info

Babylonian Society

Hammurabi's Code of Law explains much more than crimes and punishments. It also gives us a great deal of information about Babylonian society.

In Hammurabi's time, there were three social classes:

Awilum were free men who owned property. They were the highest class. *Awilum* were required to pay taxes and serve in the military. When an *awilum* died, his property went to his sons.

Muskenum were the middle class. They were free citizens, but they did not own property. *Muskenum* often served in the palace in exchange for food or, sometimes, land allotments.

Wardum were slaves, the lowest class. *Wardum* were considered property. However, they had more rights in Babylon than in other parts of the world. Once they finished their duties for their master, they could work at another job for pay. They could also do business on the side and own property. If slaves could save enough money, they could buy their freedom.

Women also had more rights than those in other societies. Their fathers usually arranged their marriages, but they still had some freedom and independence. They could have their own money and their property. Also, a woman who was abused or neglected by her husband could take her dowry and leave him.

Punishments were given out according to one's social rank. If an *awilum* lost an eye, then the attacker lost an eye. If a *muskenum*, the attacker had to pay the victim a fee. The fee was less if the victim was a *wardum*. There was another side to this, though. For many offenses, penalties were more severe for the more privileged *awilum*. Punishments for *wardum* were lighter—unless their offense was against someone in a higher class.

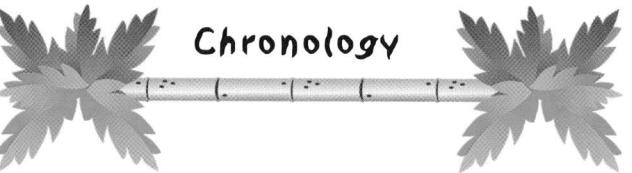

Chronology

All dates B.C.E.*

Ca. 1810	Hammurabi born in Babylon.
1792	King Sin-Muballit dies.
	Hammurabi begins his reign.
1787	Hammurabi conquers Uruk and Isin, held by Rim-Sin.
1786	Clashes with Larsa, but no resolution to conflicts.
1784	Fightings with neighbors in northwest and east; Hammurabi conquers Emutbal.
1782	Hammurabi conquers Malgia.
1776	Shamshi-Adad is killed.
1776–1768	Peaceful time; used it to fortify cities on northern borders.
1764	Hammurabi wages war against Elamite forces.
1763	War against Rim-Sin, where Hammurabi is victor.
1762	Hostilities with eastern powers, Elam and Eshnunna; Hammurabi is victor; Hammurabi attacks Mari.
1761	War against Mari in the northwest; Hammurabi is victor.
1760	War against Babylonia's neighbors in the east.
1758–1755	Directed armies eastward for third time; Mari rebelled and Hammurabi destroyed the city.
1755	Eshnunna in the north is totally defeated by Hammurabi; helped by damming the Tigris.
1753–1750	Concentrated on construction and defense fortifications.
1750	Hammurabi dies; his son Samsuiluna becomes king.

*Before the Common Era—a relatively new term expected to replace the religious dating, B.C.

Timeline in History

All dates B.C.E.*

2004	Ibbi-Sin, last king of Ur, is captured by Elamites and taken to Susa.
2000	Fall of the Sumerian Empire; Amorites interrupt trade routes; Ur attacked by Elamites and falls; Assyria becomes independent and establishes trade network in Anatolia.
1900	Amorite chiefs take over some cities as rulers.
1797	Egypt's Amenemhet III dies and is succeeded by his son, who will reign until 1783 B.C. as Amenemhet IV.
1792	Hammurabi, an Amorite ruler, becomes King of Babylon.
1783	Egypt's twelfth (Theban) dynasty ends after 208 years.
1760	Hammurabi conquers all of Mesopotamia.
1750	The great Indus Valley cities of Mohenjo-Daro and Harappa collapse.
1740	Expansion of the Hittite kingdom in Anatolia.
1700	The first real alphabet is developed by the peoples of Syria and Palestine.
1700	Babylonians use windmills to pump water for irrigation.

*Before the Common Era—a relatively new term expected to replace the religious dating, B.C.

BIOGRAPHY FROM
ANCIENT CIVILIZATIONS
LEGENDS, FOLKLORE, AND STORIES OF ANCIENT WORLDS

Chapter Notes

CHAPTER ONE   CHOSEN BY THE GODS
   1. From "Sargon, King of Battle" in Benjamin R. Foster, *From Distant Days: Myths, Tales, and Poetry of Ancient Mesopotamia*. CDL Press, 1995, p. 170.
   2. From "A Prayer for Hammurabi." Translation from *The Electronic Text Corpus of Sumerian Literature*. The Oriental Institute, University of Oxford.
   3. From "The Legend of Naram-Sin" in Benjamin R. Foster, *From Distant Days: Myths, Tales, and Poetry of Ancient Mesopotamia*. CDL Press, 1995, pp. 176–77.
   4. From the stele of Hammurabi in Nels M. Bailkey, *Readings in Ancient History: Thought and Experience from Gilgamesh to St. Augustine*. D.C. Heath, 1992, p. 31.

CHAPTER TWO   HOW WE KNOW WHAT WE KNOW
   1. Marcel Sigrist and Peter Damerow. *Mesopotamian Year Names: Neo-Sumerian and Old Babylonian Date Formulae*. Cuneiform Digital Library Initiative, University of California at Los Angeles and Max Planck Institute for the History of Science.

CHAPTER THREE   A PRACTICAL KING
   1. Translation from *The Electronic Text Corpus of Sumerian Literature*. The Oriental Institute, University of Oxford. ETCSL translation t.2.8.2.3.
   2. Marcel Sigrist and Peter Damerow. *Mesopotamian Year Names: Neo-Sumerian and Old Babylonian Date Formulae*. Cuneiform Digital Library Initiative, University of California at Los Angeles and Max Planck Institute for the History of Science.
   3. William H. Stiebing, Jr. *Ancient Near Eastern History and Culture*. Longman, 2003, p. 88.

CHAPTER FOUR   AN AMBITIOUS KING
   1. William H. Stiebing, Jr. *Ancient Near Eastern History and Culture*. Longman, 2003, p. 80.
   2. A. Leo Oppenheim. *Letters from Mesopotamia: Official, Business, and Private Letters on Clay Tablets from Two Millennia*. University of Chicago Press, 1967.
   3. Translation from *The Electronic Text Corpus of Sumerian Literature*. The Oriental Institute, University of Oxford. ETCSL translation: t.2.8.2.2.
   4. Marcel Sigrist and Peter Damerow. *Mesopotamian Year Names: Neo-Sumerian and Old Babylonian Date Formulae*. Cuneiform Digital Library Initiative, University of California at Los Angeles and Max Planck Institute for the History of Science.
   5. L. W. King. *The Letters and Inscriptions of Hammurabi, the King of Babylon, Vol. III*. Luzac and Co., 1900, pp. 14, 17.
   6. Ibid., p. 78.
   7. Ibid., p. 182.

CHAPTER FIVE   A JUST KING
   1. From "The Laws of Hammurabi" in Nels M. Bailkey, *Readings in Ancient History: Thought and Experience from Gilgamesh to St. Augustine*. D.C. Heath, 1992. From the Prologue, p. 31.
   2. A. Leo Oppenheim. *Ancient Mesopotamia: Portrait of a Dead Civilization*. University of Chicago Press, 1964, p. 157.

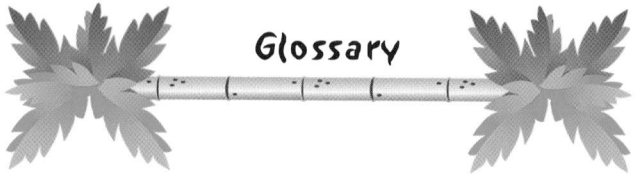

Glossary

alliance	(uh-LIE-uns)—a formal agreement to cooperate
ambassador	(am-BAS-uh-dur)—a diplomat
artisan	(AHR-ti-zun)—a person who is skilled in a craft
āšipu	(AY-sip-oo)—a doctor who uses magic or spells and chants
asû	(AY-soo)—a doctor who uses medical cures
baru	(BAH-roo)—a diviner; a fortune-teller
city-state	(SIT-ee STAYT)—a self-governing city and the land surrounding it
dais	(DAY-is)—a raised platform
diviner	(di-VIE-nur)—a person who practices fortune-telling
epilogue	(EP-uh-log)—a section added to the end of a written work
irrigation	(ear-uh-GAY-shun)—supplying water by means of channels, streams, or pipes
nomad	(NOE-mad)—a person who wanders
omen	(OE-mun)—a sign that foretells good or bad luck
prologue	(PROE-log)—a section added to the beginning of a written work
rival	(RIE-vul)—a person who competes with another
scribe	(skryb)—a person who writes or copies text as a profession
stele/stela	(STEE-lee/STEE-luh)—a column or pillar of stone carved with an inscription
ziggurat	(ZIG-uh-rat)—a tall temple tower built in stepped stages with a temple or shrine on top

For Further Reading

For Young Adults

Ali, Daud et al. *Great Civilizations of the East*. Southwater, 2001.

Chrisp, Peter. *Mesopotamia: Iraq in Ancient Times*. Enchanted Lion Books, 2004.

Kramer, Samuel Noah, et al. *Cradle of Civilization*. Time-Life Books, 1987.

Landau, Elaine. *The Babylonians*. Millbrook Press, 1997.

Oakes, Lorna. *Step into Mesopotamia*. Lorenz Books, 2001.

Oppenheim, A. Leo. *Letters from Mesopotamia*. University of Chicago Press, 1967.

Time-Life Books. *Mesopotamia: The Mighty Kings*. Time-Life Books, 1995.

Westenholz, Joan Goodnick. *Legends of the Kings of Akkade*. Eisenbrauns, 1997.

On the Internet

The British Museum: "Illuminating World Cultures: Mesopotamia"
http://www.mesopotamia.co.uk

Cuneiform Digital Library Initiative, University of California at Los Angeles and Max Planck Institute for the History of Science.
http://cdli.ucla.edu/dl/yearnames/HTML/T12K6.htm

The Electronic Text Corpus of Sumerian Literature. The Oriental Institute, University of Oxford.
http://etcsl.orinst.ox.ac.uk/cgi-bin/etcslmac.cgi?text=t.2.8.2.2#
http://etcsl.orinst.ox.ac.uk/cgi-bin/etcslmac.cgi?text=t.2.8.2.3#
http://www-etcsl.orient.ox.ac.uk/section2/tr2825.htm

Video

Ancient Mesopotamia. Schlessinger Media, 1998. Executive Producer, Andrew Schlessinger. 23 minutes.

Works Consulted

Bailkey, Nels M. *Readings in Ancient History: Thought and Experience from Gilgamesh to St. Augustine*. D.C. Heath, 1992.

Bertman, Stephen. *Handbook to Life in Ancient Mesopotamia*. Facts on File, 2003.

Foster, Benjamin R. *From Distant Days: Myths, Tales, and Poetry of Ancient Mesopotamia*. CDL Press, 1995.

Hoare, Frederick Russell. *Eight Decisive Books of Antiquity*. Books for Libraries Press, 1952.

King, L. W. *The Letters and Inscriptions of Hammurabi*. Luzac and Co., 1900.

Leick, Gwendolyn. *The Babylonians*. Routledge, 2003.

Nemet-Nejat, Karen Rhea. *Daily Life in Ancient Mesopotamia*. Greenwood Press, 1998.

Saggs, H. W. F. *Everyday Life in Babylonia and Assyria*. Dorset Press, 1965.

——. *Babylonians*. University of Oklahoma Press, 1995.

Seagle, William. *Men of Law: From Hammurabi to Holmes*. Macmillan, 1947.

Stiebing, William H., Jr. *Ancient Near Eastern History and Culture*. Longman, 2003.

Index